math
expressions
Common Core.

Dr. Karen C. Fuson

Homework and Remembering Grade 1
Volume 1

This material is based upon work supported by the
National Science Foundation
under Grant Numbers
ESI-9816320, REC-9806020, and RED-935373.

Any opinions, findings, and conclusions, or recommendations expressed in this material
are those of the author and do not necessarily reflect the views of the National Science Foundation.

HMH

Printed in the U.S.A.

ISBN 978-1-328-70260-9

12 0928 26 25 24 23

4500865344   B C D E F G

1 Write how many dots. See the 5 in each group.

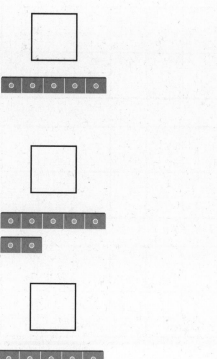 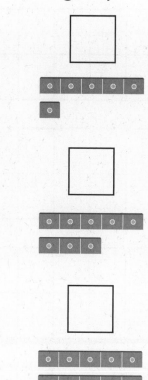

2 See the 5-group. Draw extra dots to show the number.

9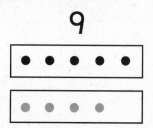

7

8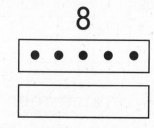

3 Write the numbers from 0–10.

| 0 | 1 | 2 | 3 | 4 | 5 | 6 | 7 | 8 | 9 | 10 |

Write the numbers.

1 | 0 | 0 | 0 | | | | | | | | | | | |
| 0 | | | | | | | | | | | | | |

2 | I | I | I | | | | | | | | | | | |
| I | | | | | | | | | | | | | |

3 | 2 | 2 | 2 | | | | | | | | | | | |
| 2 | | | | | | | | | | | | | |

4 | 3 | 3 | 3 | | | | | | | | | | | |
| 3 | | | | | | | | | | | | | |

5 | 4 | 4 | 4 | | | | | | | | | | | |
| 4 | | | | | | | | | | | | | |

6 **Stretch Your Thinking** Draw 2 flowers.

Write how many dots. See the 5 in each group.

1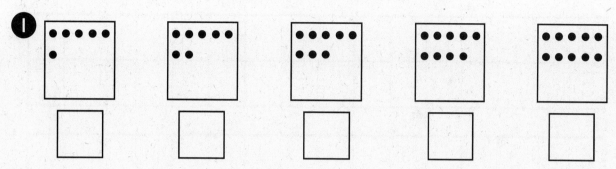

Write how many leaves. See the 5 in each row.

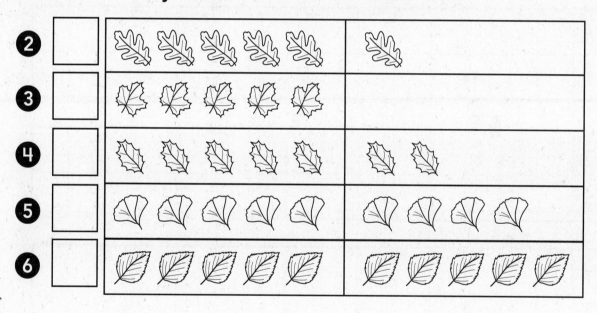

7 Write the numbers from 0–10.

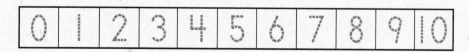

8 Explain to your Homework Helper how 5-groups help you see 6, 7, 8, 9, 10.

Write the numbers.

1 | 5 | 5 | 5 | | | | | | | | | |
| 5 | | | | | | | | | | | |

2 | 6 | 6 | 6 | | | | | | | | | |
| 6 | | | | | | | | | | | |

3 | 7 | 7 | 7 | | | | | | | | | |
| 7 | | | | | | | | | | | |

4 | 8 | 8 | 8 | | | | | | | | | |
| 8 | | | | | | | | | | | |

5 | 9 | 9 | 9 | | | | | | | | | |
| 9 | | | | | | | | | | | |

6 **Stretch Your Thinking** Draw 3 cats.

Visualize a Number as a 5-Group and Ones

Write the partners.

1 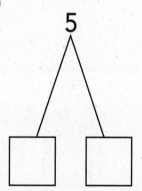 $5 = 4 + 1$

$5 = $ _____

$5 = $ _____

$5 = $ _____

2

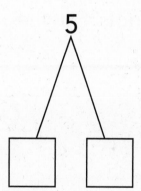 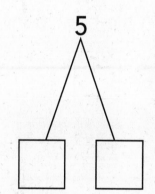

3 Write the numbers.

0	0	0										
0												

1	1	1										
1												

Write how many airplanes. See the 5 in each row.

1. [ ]
2. [ ]
3. [ ]
4. [ ]

Write how many dots. See the 5 in each group.

5. [ ]

6. [ ]

7. [ ]

8. [ ]

9. **Stretch Your Thinking** Draw 4 trees.

Partners of 2 Through 5

1 Show and write the 6-partners.

⬡ O O O O O	☐ + ☐	6 = _____
⬡ O O O O O	☐ + ☐	6 = _____
⬡ O O O O O	☐ + ☐	6 = _____
⬡ O O O O O	☐ + ☐	6 = _____
⬡ O O O O O	☐ + ☐	6 = _____

2 Write the 6-partners.

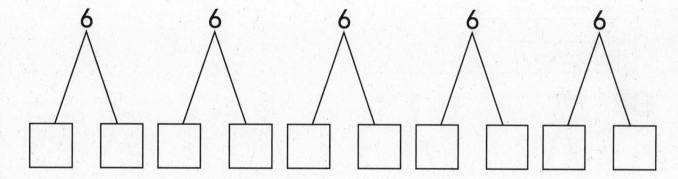

3 Write the numbers.

2	2	2											
2													

3	3	3											
3													

Write how many chickens. See the 5 in each row.

1 [ ] 🐔 🐔 🐔 🐔 🐔 | 🐔 🐔 🐔 🐔

2 [ ] 🐔 🐔 🐔 🐔 🐔 |

3 [ ] 🐤 🐤 🐤 🐤 🐤 | 🐤

Write the partners.

4 [● ● ● ● ○]   5 = 4 + 1

[● ● ● ○ ○]   5 = _____

[● ● ○ ○ ○]   5 = _____

[● ○ ○ ○ ○]   5 = _____

5

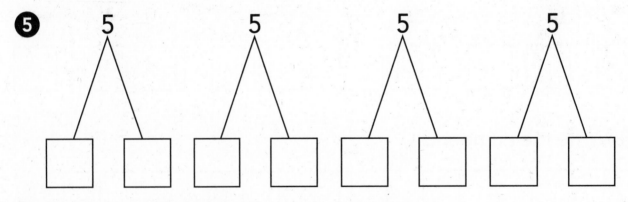

6 **Stretch Your Thinking** Draw 5 balloons.

Show the 7-partners and switch the partners.

1 | ◯◯◯◯◯◯◯ | ☐ + ☐ | and | ☐ + ☐ |

2 | ◯◯◯◯◯◯◯ | ☐ + ☐ | and | ☐ + ☐ |

3 | ◯◯◯◯◯◯◯ | ☐ + ☐ | and | ☐ + ☐ |

Write the partners and the switched partners.

4 7-train

| ☐ + ☐ | ☐ + ☐ | ☐ + ☐ |
| ☐ + ☐ | ☐ + ☐ | ☐ + ☐ |

Use patterns to solve.

5 2 + 1 = ☐   4 + 1 = ☐   5 + 1 = ☐

6 + 1 = ☐   1 + 1 = ☐   3 + 1 = ☐

6 1 + 6 = ☐   1 + 1 = ☐   1 + 2 = ☐

1 + 5 = ☐   1 + 4 = ☐   1 + 3 = ☐

Write the numbers.

7

| 4 | 4 | 4 | | | | | | | | | | |
| 4 | | | | | | | | | | | | |

8

| 5 | 5 | 5 | | | | | | | | | | |
| 5 | | | | | | | | | | | | |

Write how many dots. See the 5 in each group.

1

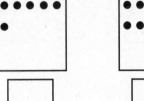 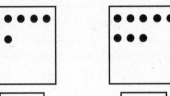 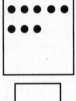 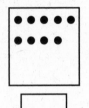 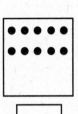

Show and write the 6-partners.

2

☐☐☐☐☐☐ | ☐ + | 6 = _____

☐☐☐☐☐☐ | ☐ + | 6 = _____

☐☐☐☐☐☐ | ☐ + | 6 = _____

☐☐☐☐☐☐ | ☐ + | 6 = _____

☐☐☐☐☐☐ | ☐ + | 6 = _____

Add.

3 $1 + 0 = \boxed{}$ $5 + 0 = \boxed{}$ $3 + 0 = \boxed{}$

4 $1 + 1 = \boxed{}$ $2 + 1 = \boxed{}$ $4 + 1 = \boxed{}$

5 **Stretch Your Thinking** Draw 6 apples. Use a 5-group.

Show the 8-partners and switch the partners.

1 ○○○○○○○○   ☐ + ☐ and ☐ + ☐

2 ○○○○○○○○   ☐ + ☐ and ☐ + ☐

3 ○○○○○○○○   ☐ + ☐ and ☐ + ☐

4 ○○○○○○○○   ☐ + ☐ and ☐ + ☐

Write the partners and the switched partners.

5 8-train

☐ + ☐   ☐ + ☐   ☐ + ☐   ☐ + ☐
☐ + ☐   ☐ + ☐   ☐ + ☐   ☐ + ☐

Use patterns to solve.

6 $8 + 0 = \boxed{}$ $5 + 0 = \boxed{}$ $0 + 4 = \boxed{}$

$0 + 6 = \boxed{}$ $0 + 2 = \boxed{}$ $0 + 7 = \boxed{}$

Write the numbers.

7

6	6	6									
6											

8

7	7	7	7	7							
7											

Write how many of each food. See the 5 in each row.

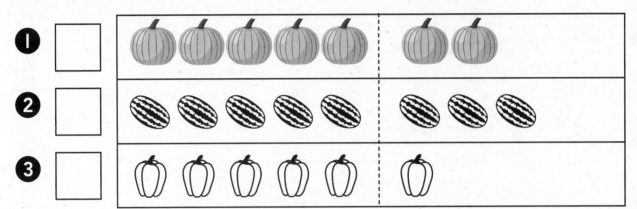

1 ☐

2 ☐

3 ☐

Show the 7-partners and switch the partners.

4 ◯◯◯◯◯◯◯   [+] and [+]

5 ◯◯◯◯◯◯◯   [+] and [+]

6 ◯◯◯◯◯◯◯   [+] and [+]

7 Write the partners and the switched partners.

7-train

+	+	+
+	+	+

8 **Stretch Your Thinking** Draw 7 fish. Use a 5-group.

Partners of 8

Name _____

Show the 9-partners and switch the partners.

1 ⬡ OOOOOOOOO | + | and | + |

2 ⬡ OOOOOOOOO | + | and | + |

3 ⬡ OOOOOOOOO | + | and | + |

4 ⬡ OOOOOOOOO | + | and | + |

Write the partners and the switched partners.

5 9-train

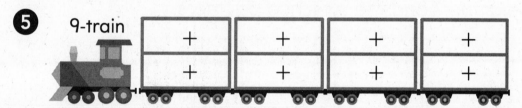

+	+	+	+
+	+	+	+

Use patterns to solve.

6 $6 - 1 = \boxed{}$ $7 - 1 = \boxed{}$ $4 - 1 = \boxed{}$

$9 - 1 = \boxed{}$ $5 - 1 = \boxed{}$ $8 - 1 = \boxed{}$

Write the numbers.

7

8	8	8												
8														

8

9	9	9												
9														

Show the 8-partners and switch the partners.

1 ⬜ ○○○○○○○○ [+] and [+]

2 ⬜ ○○○○○○○○ [+] and [+]

3 ⬜ ○○○○○○○○ [+] and [+]

4 ⬜ ○○○○○○○○ [+] and [+]

---

5 Write the partners and the switched partners.

8-train [+ / +] [+ / +] [+ / +] [+ / +]

Subtract.

6 4 − 1 = ☐   2 − 1 = ☐   3 − 1 = ☐

7 2 − 2 = ☐   5 − 2 = ☐   3 − 2 = ☐

8 **Stretch Your Thinking** Draw 8 bugs. Use a 5-group.

[ ]

Partners of 9

1 Write the 10-partners and the switched partners.

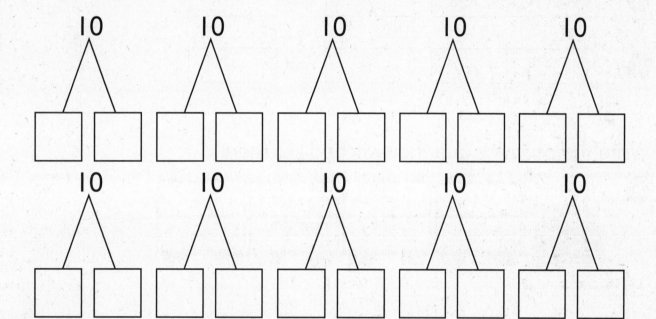

9 + 1	+	+	+	+
1 + 9	+	+	+	+

2 Use patterns to solve.

7 + 1 = ☐   9 + 1 = ☐   1 + 8 = ☐

10 − 1 = ☐   7 − 1 = ☐   9 − 1 = ☐

9 + 0 = ☐   0 + 10 = ☐   7 + 0 = ☐

8 − 0 = ☐   7 − 0 = ☐   10 − 0 = ☐

Show the 9-partners and switch the partners.

1 ⭕⭕⭕⭕⭕⭕⭕⭕⭕ | ___ + ___ | and | ___ + ___

2 ⭕⭕⭕⭕⭕⭕⭕⭕⭕ | ___ + ___ | and | ___ + ___

3 ⭕⭕⭕⭕⭕⭕⭕⭕⭕ | ___ + ___ | and | ___ + ___

4 ⭕⭕⭕⭕⭕⭕⭕⭕⭕ | ___ + ___ | and | ___ + ___

Write the partners and the switched partners.

5 9-train

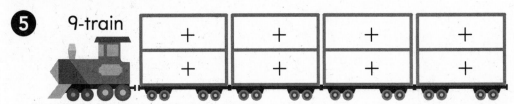

___ + ___ | ___ + ___ | ___ + ___ | ___ + ___

6 Write the numbers from 0–10.

| 0 | | | 4 | | | 7 | | | |

7 **Stretch Your Thinking** Draw 9 stars. Use a 5-group.

Partners of 10

Show and write the partners of 10.

1 10 = ____ + ____

2 10 = ____ + ____

3 10 = ____ + ____

4 10 = ____ + ____

5 10 = ____ + ____

6 10 = ____ + ____

7 10 = ____ + ____

8 10 = ____ + ____

9 10 = ____ + ____

Write the 10-partners and the switched partners.

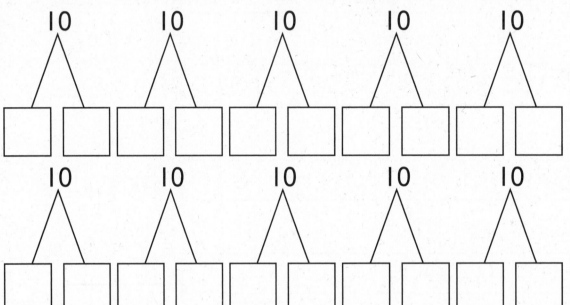

1

$$\frac{9 + 1}{1 + 9}$$

$$\frac{ + }{ + }$$

$$\frac{ + }{ + }$$

$$\frac{ + }{ + }$$

$$\frac{ + }{ + }$$

2

10   10   10   10   10

10   10   10   10   10

3 10-train

4 **Stretch Your Thinking** Draw 10 marbles.
Use 5-groups.

Focus on Mathematical Practices

Write the partners and the total.

1 ☐ + ☐

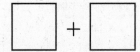

Total ☐

2 ☐ + ☐

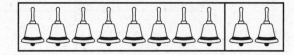

Total ☐

3 ☐ + ☐

Total ☐

4 ☐ + ☐

Total ☐

5 ☐ + ☐

Total ☐

6 ☐ + ☐

Total ☐

7 ☐ + ☐

Total ☐

8 ☐ + ☐

Total ☐

1 Write the numbers from 0–10.

2 Write how many dots. See the 5 in each group.

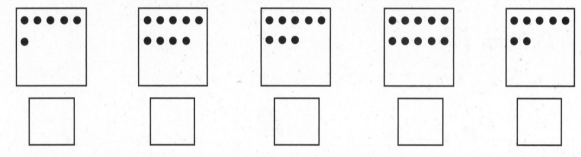

Write how many leaves. See the 5 in each row.

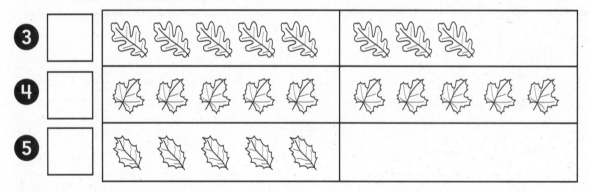

6 Write the 5-partners as a train.

5-train

7 **Stretch Your Thinking** Write partners of 7. Draw a Break-Apart Stick to show the partners. Write the total.

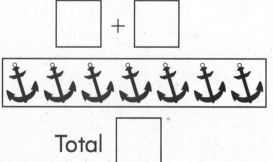

Total

Represent Addition

Name _____

Write the partners and total for each circle drawing.

1 ☐ + ☐

● ● ● ● ● ● ● ○ ○

Total ☐

2 ☐ + ☐

● ● ● ● ○ ○ ○

Total ☐

3 ☐ + ☐

● ● ● ● ● ○

Total ☐

4 ☐ + ☐

● ● ● ● ● ● ● ● ○ ○

Total ☐

5 ☐ + ☐

● ● ● ● ○ ○

Total ☐

6 ☐ + ☐

● ● ● ● ○ ○ ○ ○

Total ☐

7 ☐ + ☐

● ● ● ● ● ● ○ ○ ○

Total ☐

8 ☐ + ☐

● ● ● ● ● ● ○ ○ ○ ○ ○

Total ☐

1 Write how many dots. See the 5 in each group.

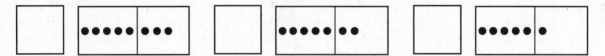

Write how many of each food. See the 5 in each row.

2

3

4

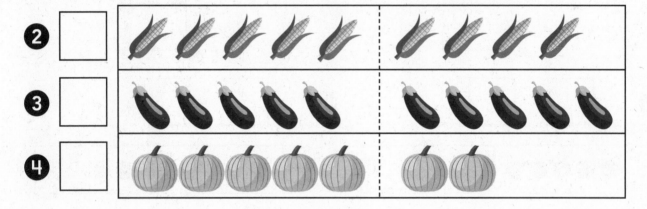

5 Write the 6-partners as a train.

6-train

6 **Stretch Your Thinking** Make a circle drawing
to show a set of partners of 10.

Addition with Circle Drawings

Name _____

Write the partners and the total. Then write the equation.

1

⬤⬤⬤⬤⬤ ⬤⬤ ◯◯

_____
Equation

Total ▭

2

⬤⬤⬤⬤⬤ ◯◯◯

_____
Equation

Total ▭

3

⬤⬤⬤⬤⬤ ⬤ ◯◯◯◯

_____
Equation

Total ▭

4

⬤⬤⬤⬤⬤ ◯◯

_____
Equation

Total ▭

1 Fill in the numbers from 0–10.

0			4	7			

Show the 7-partners and switch the partners.

2  [+] and [+]

3 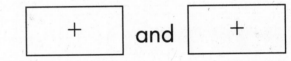 [+] and [+]

4  [+] and [+]

5 Write the partners and the switched partners.

7-train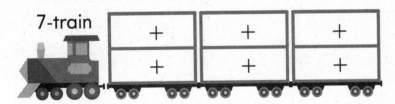

+	+	+
+	+	+

6 **Stretch Your Thinking** Make a circle drawing to match the picture. Then write the equation.

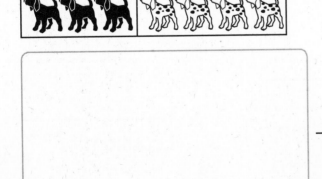

_____
Equation

Addition Equations

Name _____

Write the partners and the total. Then write the equation.

1 ☐ + ☐

●●●●● ●●● ○○

Total ☐

_____
Equation

2 ☐ + ☐

●●●●● ○○○

Total ☐

_____
Equation

3 ☐ + ☐

●●●●● ●● ○○

Total ☐

_____
Equation

4 ☐ + ☐

●●●●● ● ○

Total ☐

_____
Equation

Write how many of each food. See the 5 in each row.

1 ▢

2 ▢

3 ▢

Show the 8-partners and switch the partners.

4 ◯◯◯◯◯◯◯◯ | + | and | +

5 ◯◯◯◯◯◯◯◯ | + | and | +

6 ◯◯◯◯◯◯◯◯ | + | and | +

7 ◯◯◯◯◯◯◯◯ | + | and | +

8 Write the partners and the switched partners.

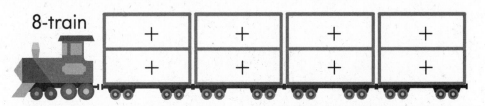

8-train | + + + + | + + + +

9 **Stretch Your Thinking** Write an equation to match the circle drawing.

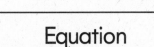

_____
Equation

Addition Equations and Stories

Name _____

Count on. Write the total.

1 | 5 ● ● ● ● = | Total ☐

2 | 7 ● ● ● = | Total ☐

3 | 3 ● ● ● ● ● = | Total ☐

4 | 6 ● ● ● = | Total ☐

5 | 4  = | Total ☐

6 | 5  = | Total ☐

7 | 2 = | Total ☐

8 | 4 = | Total ☐

9 | 5 = | Total ☐

10 | 8 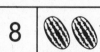 = | Total ☐

11 | 6  = | Total ☐

12 | 3  = | Total ☐

Name _____

Show the 9-partners and switch the partners.

1 ⭕⭕⭕⭕⭕⭕⭕⭕⭕ [+] and [+]

2 ⭕⭕⭕⭕⭕⭕⭕⭕⭕ [+] and [+]

3 ⭕⭕⭕⭕⭕⭕⭕⭕⭕ [+] and [+]

4 ⭕⭕⭕⭕⭕⭕⭕⭕⭕ [+] and [+]

5 Write the partners and the switched partners.

9-train

| + | + | + | + |
| + | + | + | + |

Use patterns to solve.

6 $0 + 9 = \boxed{}$ $6 + 0 = \boxed{}$ $0 + 7 = \boxed{}$

7 $8 - 0 = \boxed{}$ $2 - 0 = \boxed{}$ $10 - 0 = \boxed{}$

8 $1 + 4 = \boxed{}$ $9 + 1 = \boxed{}$ $5 + 1 = \boxed{}$

9 **Stretch Your Thinking** Count on to find

the total. $7 + 2 = \boxed{}$

Now count all. Did you get the same answer? Explain.

_____

Explore Solution Methods

Count on to find the total.

1 6 + 3 = ☐   **2** 3 + 5 = ☐   **3** 4 + 5 = ☐

4 5 + 5 = ☐   **5** 4 + 6 = ☐   **6** 2 + 4 = ☐

7 4 + 3 = ☐   **8** 7 + 2 = ☐   **9** 6 + 2 = ☐

Find the total number of toys.

10 7 horns in the box

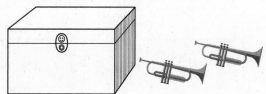

☐ Total

11 5 bears in the box

☐ Total

12 3 balls in the box

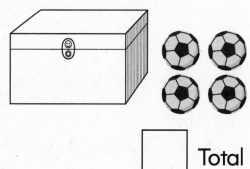

☐ Total

13 8 train cars in the box

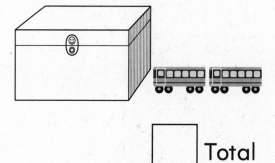

☐ Total

1 Fill in the numbers from 0–10.

	1		4		6	7			

Show the 10-partners and switch the partners.

2    [+] and [+]

3    [+] and [+]

4    [+] and [+]

5 ○○○○○○○○○○   [+] and [+]

6 ○○○○○○○○○○   [+] and [+]

7 **Stretch Your Thinking** Count on with dots to find the total. Write the total.

6 + 3 = ☐

Addition Strategies: Counting On

Underline the greater number.
Count on from that number.

1 $\overset{\bullet\bullet\bullet}{3} + \underline{6} = \boxed{}$

2 $2 + 5 = \boxed{}$

3 $2 + 8 = \boxed{}$

4 $7 + 3 = \boxed{}$

5 $4 + 5 = \boxed{}$

6 $3 + 5 = \boxed{}$

7 $2 + 7 = \boxed{}$

8 $6 + 4 = \boxed{}$

9 $4 + 3 = \boxed{}$

10 $2 + 6 = \boxed{}$

11 $8 + 2 = \boxed{}$

12 $6 + 3 = \boxed{}$

Name _____

Write the partners and the total.

1 ☐ + ☐

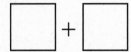

Total ☐

2 ☐ + ☐

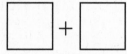

Total ☐

3 ☐ + ☐

Total ☐

4 ☐ + ☐

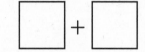

Total ☐

Use patterns to solve.

5 $8 - 1 =$ ☐ $4 - 1 =$ ☐ $10 - 1 =$ ☐

6 $0 + 5 =$ ☐ $0 + 9 =$ ☐ $7 + 0 =$ ☐

7 $10 - 0 =$ ☐ $5 - 0 =$ ☐ $6 - 0 =$ ☐

8 **Stretch Your Thinking** Sami counts on to solve
this problem. $2 + 8 =$ ☐
Sami counts 8, 9 and says the total is 9. What did
she do wrong?

Count On from the Greater Number

Underline the greater number.
Count on from that number.

1 $\overset{\bullet\bullet}{2} + \underline{7} = \boxed{}$

2 $1 + 9 = \boxed{}$

3 $3 + 4 = \boxed{}$

4 $6 + 3 = \boxed{}$

5 $4 + 5 = \boxed{}$

6 $3 + 7 = \boxed{}$

7 $2 + 4 = \boxed{}$

8 $5 + 3 = \boxed{}$

9 $8 + 2 = \boxed{}$

10 $5 + 2 = \boxed{}$

11 $3 + 6 = \boxed{}$

12 $6 + 2 = \boxed{}$

13 $2 + 8 = \boxed{}$

14 $7 + 3 = \boxed{}$

Write the partners and the total.

1 ☐ + ☐

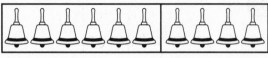

Total ☐

2 ☐ + ☐

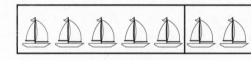

Total ☐

3 ☐ + ☐

Total ☐

4 ☐ + ☐

Total ☐

Write the partners and total for each circle drawing.

5 ☐ + ☐

● ● ● ● ● ● | ● ● ● ○ ○

Total ☐

6 ☐ + ☐

● ● ● ● ● | ○ ○ ○

Total ☐

7 **Stretch Your Thinking** Ring the greater number and count on from that number.

Write the total.

$4 + 5 =$ ☐

Addition Game: Unknown Totals

Underline the greater number.
Count on from that number.

1 ••••
$4 + \underline{5} =$ ☐

2 $6 + 3 =$ ☐

3 $3 + 5 =$ ☐

4 $2 + 3 =$ ☐

5 $2 + 8 =$ ☐

6 $4 + 2 =$ ☐

7 $4 + 3 =$ ☐

8 $7 + 3 =$ ☐

9 $8 + 2 =$ ☐

10 $6 + 2 =$ ☐

11 $3 + 7 =$ ☐

12 $5 + 2 =$ ☐

13 $2 + 7 =$ ☐

14 $7 + 2 =$ ☐

Write the partners and total for each circle drawing.

1  ⬜ + ⬜

●●●●● | ○○

Total ⬜

2 ⬜ + ⬜

●●● | ○○ ○

Total ⬜

3 ⬜ + ⬜

●●●●● ●●● | ○○

Total ⬜

4 ⬜ + ⬜

●●●●● ● | ○○○○

Total ⬜

Write the partners and the total. Then write the equation.

5 ⬜ + ⬜

●●●●● ●● | ○○

Total ⬜

_____
Equation

6 **Stretch Your Thinking** Write an addition
equation. Draw dots to count on to solve it.

Practice Counting On

Name _____

Solve. Write how many are left.

1 There are 7 boats.

$7 - 4 =$ ☐

Then 4 sail away.

---

2 There are 10 candles.

$10 - 7 =$ ☐

Then 7 go out.

---

3 There are 8 muffins.

$8 - 6 =$ ☐

Then 6 are eaten.

---

4 There are 9 fish.

$9 - 5 =$ ☐

Then 5 swim away.

---

5 There are 6 elephants.

$6 - 4 =$ ☐

Then 4 go away.

Write the partners and the total. Then write the equation.

1

Total [ ]   _____
    Equation

2

Total [ ]   _____
    Equation

3

Total [ ]   _____
    Equation

4 **Stretch Your Thinking** Write an equation
for this story problem. There are 8 ants.
Then 2 crawl away.

_____
Equation

Represent Subtraction

Name _____

Subtract and write the equation.

1 ⓵ ◯◯◯◯◯ ◯◯◯◯

Subtract 3

_____
Equation

2 ◯◯◯◯◯ ◯

Subtract 5

_____
Equation

3 ◯◯◯◯◯ ◯◯◯◯◯

Subtract 3

_____
Equation

4 ◯◯◯◯◯ ◯◯

Subtract 4

_____
Equation

5 ◯◯◯◯◯ ◯◯◯◯

Subtract 4

_____
Equation

6 ◯◯◯◯◯ ◯◯◯◯

Subtract 6

_____
Equation

Name _____

Write the partners and the total. Then write the equation.

1 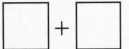 +

_____
Equation

Total [ ]

2 [ ] + [ ]

_____
Equation

Total [ ]

Count on. Write the total.

3 Total

| 5 | ● ● ● ● | = [ ] |

4 Total

| 7 | ● ● ● | = [ ] |

5 Total

| 3 | ● ● ● ● ● | = [ ] |

6 Total

| 6 | ● ● ● | = [ ] |

7 **Stretch Your Thinking** Make a circle drawing.
Then write the equation to solve. There are
6 butterflies. 4 fly away. How many are left?

_____
Equation

Subtraction with Drawings and Equations

Name _____

Use the picture to solve the equation.

1

$$10 - 7 = \boxed{}$$

2

$$7 - 2 = \boxed{}$$

3

$$9 - 6 = \boxed{}$$

4

$$8 - 4 = \boxed{}$$

5

$$5 - 3 = \boxed{}$$

6

$$6 - 2 = \boxed{}$$

7

$$7 - 4 = \boxed{}$$

8

$$9 - 4 = \boxed{}$$

9

$$6 - 4 = \boxed{}$$

10

$$8 - 5 = \boxed{}$$

11

$$10 - 8 = \boxed{}$$

12

$$7 - 7 = \boxed{}$$

Name _____

Count on. Write the total.

1    Total

| 3 | 🍎🍎🍎🍎 | = | ☐ |

2    Total

| 5 | | = | ☐ |

3 Total

| 2 | 🍓🍓🍓🍓🍓 | = | ☐ |

4 Total

| 4 | 🍆🍆 | = | ☐ |

Find the total number of toys.

5 8 horns in the box

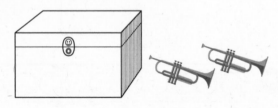

☐ Total

6 7 train cars in the box

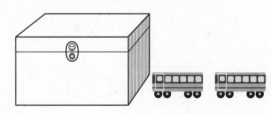

☐ Total

7 **Stretch Your Thinking** Make a circle drawing
to show subtraction. Then write the equation.

```


```

_____
Equation

Practice with Subtraction

Use the circles to solve the equation.

1 ⭕⭕⭕⭕ ⭕⭕⭕⭕

$9 - 5 =$ ☐

2 ⭕⭕⭕⭕ ⭕

$6 - 2 =$ ☐

3 ⭕⭕⭕⭕⭕ ⭕⭕⭕⭕

$10 - 8 =$ ☐

4 ⭕⭕⭕⭕⭕ ⭕⭕⭕

$8 - 5 =$ ☐

5 ⭕⭕⭕⭕⭕ ⭕

$6 - 3 =$ ☐

6 ⭕⭕⭕⭕⭕

$5 - 2 =$ ☐

7 ⭕⭕⭕⭕⭕ ⭕⭕

$7 - 3 =$ ☐

8 ⭕⭕⭕⭕⭕ ⭕⭕⭕⭕

$9 - 6 =$ ☐

Solve the equation.

9 $6 - 4 =$ ☐

10 $8 - 6 =$ ☐

11 $10 - 2 =$ ☐

12 $7 - 1 =$ ☐

13 $9 - 7 =$ ☐

14 $8 - 4 =$ ☐

Name _____

Find the total number of toys.

1 4 balls in the box

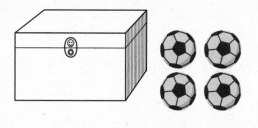

[ ] Total

2 6 bears in the box

[ ] Total

Underline the greater number.
Count on from that number.

3 ••• $\underline{6} + 3 =$ [ ]

4 $2 + 5 =$ [ ]

5 $2 + 6 =$ [ ]

6 $7 + 2 =$ [ ]

7 $3 + 7 =$ [ ]

8 $3 + 5 =$ [ ]

9 **Stretch Your Thinking** Use a circle drawing
to solve this equation. Show your work.

$8 - 5 = 3$

Generate Subtraction Problems

Name _____

Use addition to solve subtraction.

1 $5 + 5 = 10$, so I know $10 - 5 = \boxed{}$.

2 $6 + 4 = 10$, so I know $10 - 4 = \boxed{}$.

3 $3 + 6 = 9$, so I know $9 - 3 = \boxed{}$.

Solve the vertical form. Use any method.

4 $\begin{array}{r} 2 \\ +\,5 \\ \hline \end{array}$ **5** $\begin{array}{r} 4 \\ +\,5 \\ \hline \end{array}$ **6** $\begin{array}{r} 7 \\ +\,1 \\ \hline \end{array}$ **7** $\begin{array}{r} 2 \\ +\,8 \\ \hline \end{array}$ **8** $\begin{array}{r} 4 \\ +\,3 \\ \hline \end{array}$

9 $\begin{array}{r} 3 \\ +\,5 \\ \hline \end{array}$ **10** $\begin{array}{r} 8 \\ +\,1 \\ \hline \end{array}$ **11** $\begin{array}{r} 1 \\ +\,9 \\ \hline \end{array}$ **12** $\begin{array}{r} 6 \\ +\,3 \\ \hline \end{array}$ **13** $\begin{array}{r} 5 \\ +\,4 \\ \hline \end{array}$

Solve the vertical form. Think about addition.

14 $\begin{array}{r} 10 \\ -\,9 \\ \hline \end{array}$ **15** $\begin{array}{r} 8 \\ -\,6 \\ \hline \end{array}$ **16** $\begin{array}{r} 9 \\ -\,1 \\ \hline \end{array}$ **17** $\begin{array}{r} 7 \\ -\,2 \\ \hline \end{array}$ **18** $\begin{array}{r} 10 \\ -\,3 \\ \hline \end{array}$

19 $\begin{array}{r} 9 \\ -\,7 \\ \hline \end{array}$ **20** $\begin{array}{r} 8 \\ -\,1 \\ \hline \end{array}$ **21** $\begin{array}{r} 7 \\ -\,4 \\ \hline \end{array}$ **22** $\begin{array}{r} 8 \\ -\,3 \\ \hline \end{array}$ **23** $\begin{array}{r} 9 \\ -\,6 \\ \hline \end{array}$

Underline the greater number.
Count on from that number.

1 $\overset{\bullet\bullet\bullet}{3} + \underline{7} = \square$

2 $6 + \overset{\bullet\bullet}{2} = \square$

3 $2 + 5 = \square$

4 $5 + 4 = \square$

5 $6 + 3 = \square$

6 $2 + 8 = \square$

7 $9 + 1 = \square$

8 $4 + 3 = \square$

9 $2 + 6 = \square$

10 $7 + 2 = \square$

11 $3 + 4 = \square$

12 $5 + 3 = \square$

13 $4 + 6 = \square$

14 $1 + 7 = \square$

15 **Stretch Your Thinking** Write the addition you
can use to solve the subtraction. Then solve.

$10 - 3 = \square$ $\square + \square = \square$

Relate Addition and Subtraction

Count on to add.

1 4 + 2 = ☐

2 3 + 5 = ☐

3 6 + 2 = ☐

4 6
    + 3

5 5
    + 5

6 2
    + 7

7 3
    + 4

8 4
    + 4

Subtract. Make a circle drawing if you wish.

9 9 − 2 = ☐

10 7 − 5 = ☐

11 6 − 3 = ☐

12 6
     − 2

13 9
     − 5

14 10
     − 7

15 5
     − 4

16 8
     − 2

Solve. Write how many are left.

1 There are 9 candles.

$9 - 7 = \boxed{}$

Then 7 go out.

2 There are 8 boats.

$8 - 4 = \boxed{}$

Then 4 sail away.

Subtract and write the equation.

3

_____
Equation

Subtract 4

4 ◯◯◯◯◯ ◯◯

_____
Equation

Subtract 2

5 **Stretch Your Thinking** Write numbers to complete the subtraction.

$\boxed{} - \boxed{} = 5$

Mixed Practice with Equations

Name _____

Draw a picture to show the story.
Write and solve the equation.

Karl sees 2 owls and 5 eagles in a park.

How many birds does he see?

$2 + 5 = \boxed{}$

Name _____

Use the circles to solve the equation.

1  **2**

$$10 - 4 = \boxed{}$$

$$9 - 2 = \boxed{}$$

Use addition to solve subtraction.

3 $7 + 3 = 10$, so I know $10 - 3 = \boxed{}$.

4 $9 + 1 = 10$, so I know $10 - 1 = \boxed{}$.

5 $4 + 5 = \boxed{}$, so I know $9 - 4 = \boxed{}$.

Solve the vertical form. Think about addition.

6 $\begin{array}{r} 6 \\ -1 \\ \hline \end{array}$
  7 $\begin{array}{r} 8 \\ -4 \\ \hline \end{array}$
  8 $\begin{array}{r} 9 \\ -7 \\ \hline \end{array}$
  9 $\begin{array}{r} 10 \\ -3 \\ \hline \end{array}$
  10 $\begin{array}{r} 7 \\ -6 \\ \hline \end{array}$

11 **Stretch Your Thinking**

Solve.

If I know $7 - 4 = \boxed{}$,

then I know $\boxed{} + \boxed{} = \boxed{}$.

Focus on Mathematical Practices

Find the unknown partner.

1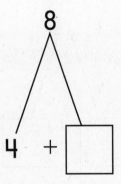
8
4 + ☐

2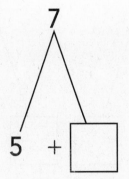
7
5 + ☐

3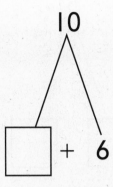
10
☐ + 6

4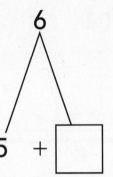
6
5 + ☐

5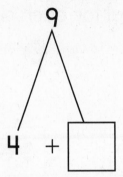
9
4 + ☐

6
10
☐ + 7

7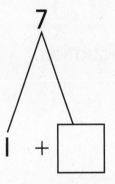
7
1 + ☐

8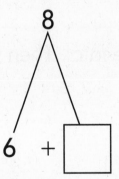
8
6 + ☐

9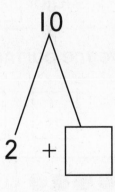
10
2 + ☐

10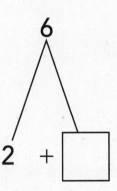
6
2 + ☐

11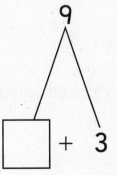
9
☐ + 3

12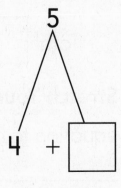
5
4 + ☐

Write the partners.

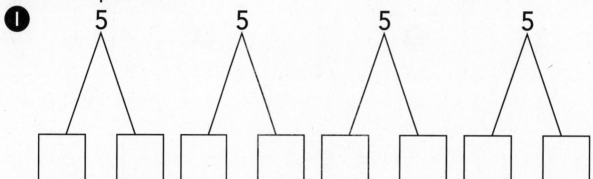

Write the partners and total for each circle drawing.

2

Total [ ]

3

Total [ ]

Write the partners and the total. Then write the equation.

4

_____
Equation

Total [ ]

5 **Stretch Your Thinking** Write an addition

equation to help solve $9 - 2 = \boxed{}$.

Name _____

Solve the story problem.

Show your work. Use drawings, numbers, or words.

1 I see 8 bees in the sky.

5 fly low. The others fly high.

How many bees fly high?

☐ _____
   label

bee

2 7 cars are in the parking lot.

Then more cars come.

Now there are 9.

How many more cars come?

☐ _____
   label

parking lot

Find the unknown partner.

3 7

5 + ☐

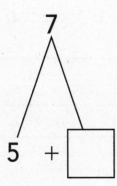

4 10

☐ + 3

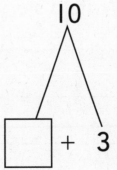

5 9

6 + ☐

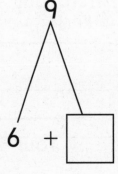

Show and write the 6-partners.

1

○○○○○○	+	$6 = 5 + 1$
○○○○○○	+	$6 = $ _____
○○○○○○	+	$6 = $ _____
○○○○○○	+	$6 = $ _____
○○○○○○	+	$6 = $ _____

Find the unknown partner.

2

$$\boxed{} + 6$$

3

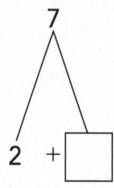

$$2 + \boxed{}$$

4

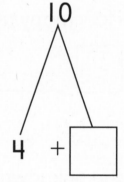

$$4 + \boxed{}$$

5 **Stretch Your Thinking** Write a story problem for Exercise 4.

_____

_____

_____

_____

Name _____

Count on to find the unknown partner.

1 $3 + \boxed{} = 7$ **2** $5 + \boxed{} = 10$ **3** $2 + \boxed{} = 6$

4 $4 + \boxed{} = 8$ **5** $7 + \boxed{} = 9$ **6** $5 + \boxed{} = 9$

7 $6 + \boxed{} = 9$ **8** $4 + \boxed{} = 10$ **9** $4 + \boxed{} = 7$

Count on to find the number of animals in the barn.

10 8 total

$\boxed{}$ in the barn

11 9 total

$\boxed{}$ in the barn

12 10 total

$\boxed{}$ in the barn

13 7 total

$\boxed{}$ in the barn

Write the partners and the switched partners.

1 7-train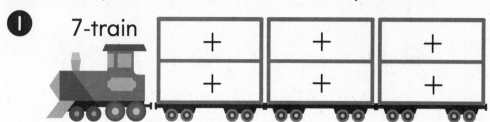

Count on. Write the total.

2 Total

 = ☐

3 Total

5 🍎🍎 = ☐

4 Total

2 🍑🍑🍑🍑 = ☐

5 Total

8 = ☐

Solve the story problem.

Show your work. Use drawings, numbers, or words.

6 Ben sees 9 ducks in the pond.
3 are white. The others are black.
How many ducks are black?

duck

☐ _____
    label

7 **Stretch Your Thinking** Write three addition equations with a total of 10.

_____

Solve Equations with Unknown Partners

Count on to find the unknown partner.

1 6 + ☐ = 9   **2** 5 + ☐ = 7   **3** 8 + ☐ = 9

4 3 + ☐ = 8   **5** 7 + ☐ = 10   **6** 4 + ☐ = 8

Solve the story problem.

Show your work. Use drawings, numbers, or words.

7 We make 10 pumpkin pies today.

6 pies are hot.

The rest are cold.

How many pies are cold?

pumpkin

☐ _____
     label

8 I have 4 kites.

Then I buy more.

Now I have 7 kites.

How many kites do I buy?

kite

☐ _____
     label

Show the 8-partners and switch the partners.

1

○○○○○○○○	+	and	+
○○○○○○○○	+	and	+
○○○○○○○○	+	and	+
○○○○○○○○	+	and	+

Add.

2 $2 + 5 = \boxed{}$ **3** $2 + 4 = \boxed{}$ **4** $8 + 2 = \boxed{}$

5 $2 + 8 = \boxed{}$ **6** $7 + 2 = \boxed{}$ **7** $5 + 2 = \boxed{}$

Subtract.

8 $5 - 2 = \boxed{}$ **9** $9 - 2 = \boxed{}$ **10** $7 - 2 = \boxed{}$

11 $8 - 2 = \boxed{}$ **12** $6 - 2 = \boxed{}$ **13** $10 - 2 = \boxed{}$

14 **Stretch Your Thinking** Write an addition equation with 3 as the unknown partner.

_____

Addition Game: Unknown Partners

Count on to find the unknown partner.

1 $5 + \boxed{} = 7$ **2** $3 + \boxed{} = 9$ **3** $4 + \boxed{} = 7$

4 $4 + \boxed{} = 8$ **5** $6 + \boxed{} = 10$ **6** $5 + \boxed{} = 9$

Solve the story problem.

Show your work. Use drawings, numbers, or words.

7 Amanda picks 2 melons at the farm.

Rosa also picks some.

Together they pick 7 melons.

How many does Rosa pick?

$\boxed{}$ _____
  label

farm

8 I have 10 masks.

7 masks are black.

The others are white.

How many masks are white?

$\boxed{}$ _____
  label

mask

Name _____

Show the 9-partners and switch the partners.

1. ⭕⭕⭕⭕⭕⭕⭕⭕⭕ [+] and [+]

    ⭕⭕⭕⭕⭕⭕⭕⭕⭕ [+] and [+]

    ⭕⭕⭕⭕⭕⭕⭕⭕⭕ [+] and [+]

    ⭕⭕⭕⭕⭕⭕⭕⭕⭕ [+] and [+]

Underline the greater number.
Count on from that number.

2. $3 + 7 = \boxed{}$ 3. $5 + 3 = \boxed{}$

4. $7 + 2 = \boxed{}$ 5. $3 + 6 = \boxed{}$

Count on to find the unknown partner.

6. $3 + \boxed{} = 10$ 7. $4 + \boxed{} = 6$ 8. $2 + \boxed{} = 9$

9. $4 + \boxed{} = 7$ 10. $3 + \boxed{} = 8$ 11. $4 + \boxed{} = 10$

12. **Stretch Your Thinking** Sal has 6 balloons.
    He buys some more. Then he has 10 balloons.
    How many balloons does Sal buy?

    _____ balloons

Practice with Unknown Partners

Name _____

Count on to solve.

1 6 − 4 = ☐   **2** 10 − 7 = ☐   **3** 8 − 3 = ☐

4   9
      − 5
      ———

5   8
      − 5
      ———

6   7
      − 3
      ———

Solve the story problem.

Show your work. Use drawings, numbers, or words.

7 6 bowls are on a tray.
We take 3 away.
How many bowls are left?

tray

☐ _____
       label

8 I see 10 bugs on the step.
6 of them fly away.
How many bugs are still there?

bug

☐ _____
       label

Write the 10-partners and the switched partners.

1 ●●●●● ●●●●● ●●●●● ●●●●● ●●●●●
  ●●●●○ ●●●○○ ●●○○○ ●○○○○ ○○○○○

$$\frac{9+1}{1+9}\qquad \frac{+}{+}\qquad \frac{+}{+}\qquad \frac{+}{+}\qquad \frac{+}{+}$$

Underline the greater number.
Count on from that number.

2 $5 + 2 = \boxed{}$

3 $8 + 2 = \boxed{}$

4 $3 + 5 = \boxed{}$

5 $3 + 7 = \boxed{}$

Show your work. Use drawings, numbers, or words.

Solve the story problem.

6 Kate has 2 books. She buys some more. Then she has 9 books. How many books does Kate buy?

book

$\boxed{}$ _____
label

7 **Stretch Your Thinking** Look at the story problem above. Does the answer need a label to make sense? Explain.

_____

_____

Subtraction Strategies

Name _____

Count on to solve.

1 8 – 4 = ☐   **2** 10 – 6 = ☐   **3** 7 – 5 = ☐

4   9
      – 4
      ‾‾‾‾

5   5
      – 3
      ‾‾‾‾

6   7
      – 2
      ‾‾‾‾

Solve the story problem.

Show your work. Use drawings, numbers, or words.

7 10 people are on the bus.
Then 7 of them get off.
How many people are on
the bus now?

bus

☐ _____
          label

8 Dan has 10 shells in his bag.
Then he gives away 3 shells.
How many shells does he
have now?

shell

☐ _____
          label

Subtract.

❶ 8 − 1 = ☐   **❷** 3 − 1 = ☐   **❸** 10 − 1 = ☐

❹ 7 − 0 = ☐   **❺** 4 − 0 = ☐   **❻** 9 − 0 = ☐

Use doubles to solve.

❼ 2 + 2 = ☐   **❽** 5 + 5 = ☐   **❾** 4 + 4 = ☐

❿ 4 − 2 = ☐   **⓫** 10 − 5 = ☐   **⓬** 8 − 4 = ☐

Solve the story problem.

Show your work. Use drawings, numbers, or words.

⓭ I have 10 buttons. 8 are black. The others are red. How many buttons are red?

☐ _____
      label

button

⓮ **Stretch Your Thinking** Draw a Math Mountain to solve Problem 13.

Subtraction Stories and Games

Name _____

Count on to solve.

1 6 − 4 = ☐   **2** 9 − 5 = ☐   **3** 8 − 2 = ☐

4 10
      − 3
      ——

5   7
      − 3
      ——

6   9
      − 6
      ——

Solve the story problem.

Show your work. Use drawings, numbers, or words.

---

7 7 girls are playing. 3 are jumping rope. The rest are on the swings. How many girls are on the swings?

swing

☐ _____

      label

---

8 I see 9 bats in a tree. Then 2 of them fly away. How many bats are left?

bat

☐ _____

      label

Name _____

Underline the greater number.
Count on from that number.

1 $3 + 6 =$ ☐

2 $3 + 2 =$ ☐

3 $5 + 2 =$ ☐

4 $2 + 8 =$ ☐

Count on to solve.

5 $8 - 5 =$ ☐

6 $7 - 3 =$ ☐

7 $10 - 8 =$ ☐

8 $\begin{array}{r} 7 \\ -\ 4 \\ \hline \end{array}$

9 $\begin{array}{r} 6 \\ -\ 4 \\ \hline \end{array}$

10 $\begin{array}{r} 9 \\ -\ 5 \\ \hline \end{array}$

Solve the story problem.

Show your work. Use drawings, numbers, or words.

11 9 children are playing tag.
Then 6 children are out.
How many children are
playing tag now?

children

☐ _____
            label

12 **Stretch Your Thinking** Write an equation
for Problem 11.

Practice with Subtraction Stories

Name _____

Solve. Watch the signs.

1 $4 + 5 = \boxed{}$ **2** $5 + \boxed{} = 8$ **3** $\boxed{} + 4 = 7$

4 $8 - 3 = \boxed{}$ **5** $10 - \boxed{} = 5$ **6** $\boxed{} - 6 = 3$

Solve the story problem.

Show your work. Use drawings, numbers, or words.

---

7 A squirrel finds 6 nuts.
He eats 2 of them.
How many nuts are left?

$\boxed{}$ _____
      label

squirrel

---

8 Mia has 8 flowers. She gives
some away. 5 flowers are left.
How many does she give away?

$\boxed{}$ _____
      label

flower

---

9 Vito has 7 grapes. He gets some
more grapes. Now he has 10 grapes.
How many grapes does he get?

$\boxed{}$ _____
      label

grapes

Count on to solve.

1 8
    − 2

2 5
    − 4

3 10
    − 3

4 9
    − 5

5 6
    − 4

6 7
    − 3

Solve. Write how many are left.

7 There are 8 fish.

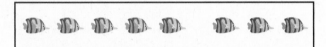

    Then 5 swim away.

Solve the story problem.

$8 - 5 = \boxed{}$

Show your work. Use drawings, numbers, or words.

---

8 I see 8 birds in a tree. Then 4 birds fly away. How many birds are left?

bird

$\boxed{}$ _____
          label

9 **Stretch Your Thinking** Complete the problem. Then write an equation to solve it. Jake has 6 toy trucks. Some are big. 2 are small.

_____

_____

Relate Addition and Subtraction Situations

Name _____

Solve. Watch the signs.

1 3 + 7 = [ ]   **2** 6 + [ ] = 9   **3** [ ] + 2 = 7

4 7 − 2 = [ ]   **5** 8 − [ ] = 4   **6** [ ] − 2 = 8

Solve the story problem.   Show your work. Use drawings, numbers, or words.

7 I see 8 clouds in the sky.
Then 6 clouds float away.
How many clouds are left?

[ ] _____
   label

cloud

8 We see 5 butterflies on the fence. Then
some land on a rock. Now there are 9
butterflies. How many land on the rock?

[ ] _____
   label

fence

9 Some boats are at the dock. Then 4 sail
away. Now there are 6 boats. How many
boats were there before?

[ ] _____
   label

boat

Name _____

Subtract and write the equation.

1 ⬭⬭⬭⬭⬭ ⬭⬭⬭⬭⬭

Subtract 4

_____
Equation

2 ⬭⬭⬭⬭⬭ ⬭⬭⬭⬭

Subtract 5

_____
Equation

Find the number of animals in the barn.

3 8 total

⬜ in the barn

4 10 total

⬜ in the barn

Solve. Watch the signs.

5 $5 + 4 = \boxed{}$ **6** $7 + \boxed{} = 10$ **7** $\boxed{} + 2 = 10$

8 $8 - 4 = \boxed{}$ **9** $7 - \boxed{} = 4$ **10** $\boxed{} - 2 = 4$

11 **Stretch Your Thinking** How did you solve Exercise 6?

_____

Solve Mixed Problems

Solve. Watch the signs.

1 $3 + 6 = \boxed{}$ **2** $5 + \boxed{} = 9$ **3** $\boxed{} + 2 = 7$

4 $7 - 4 = \boxed{}$ **5** $10 - \boxed{} = 7$ **6** $\boxed{} - 5 = 3$

Solve the story problem.

Show your work. Use drawings, numbers, or words.

7 We see some zebras. 6 of them leave. Now there are 2 zebras. How many zebras are there at first?

zebra

$\boxed{}$ _____

label

8 Tim had 10 toy cars in his room. Then he gives some away. Now there are 4. How many toy cars does he give away?

toy car

$\boxed{}$ _____

label

9 Zoe has 4 pencils in her desk. She gets some more pencils. Now she has 9 pencils. How many pencils does she get?

desk

$\boxed{}$ _____

label

Name _____

Add.

1   8
     + 2

2   3
     + 7

3   1
     + 9

4   6
     + 4

5   5
     + 5

6   4
     + 6

Count on to find the unknown partner.

7 8 + ☐ = 10   **8** 2 + ☐ = 7   **9** 9 + ☐ = 10

10 5 + ☐ = 7   **11** 7 + ☐ = 10   **12** 4 + ☐ = 8

Show your work. Use drawings, numbers, or words.

Solve the story problem.

13 I see 9 cars in the lot.
Then 4 cars drive away.
How many cars are left?

☐ _____
        label

car

14 **Stretch Your Thinking** Sal writes the equation

$4 + \boxed{5} = 9$ to solve Problem 13.

Write a subtraction equation to solve the problem.

_____

Practice with Mixed Problems

Use the picture to write a story problem.
Write and solve the equation.

_____

- -

_____

- -

_____

- -

_____

- -

_____

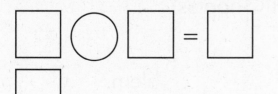

label

Name _____

Solve the story problem.

Show your work. Use drawings, numbers, or words.

---

1 Yolanda has 9 cats. 2 are black. The others are white. How many cats are white?

cat

☐ _____

label

---

2 5 lemons are on a tray. We take away 3. How many lemons are left?

tray

☐ _____

label

---

3 I have 8 CDs. I buy some more CDs. Now I have 10 CDs. How many CDs do I buy?

CD

☐ _____

label

---

4 **Stretch Your Thinking** Fill in the numbers to make your own problem. Then solve.

I have ☐ apples.

I buy some more. Now I have ☐ apples.

How many apples do I buy?

☐ _____

label

Focus on Mathematical Practices

How many stars? Count by tens.

1

___ ___ ___ ___ ___ ___ ___ Total

Add 1 ten.

2

$+$

$60 + 10 = \boxed{}$

3

$+$

$20 + 10 = \boxed{}$

4 $80 + 10 = \boxed{}$

5 $90 + 10 = \boxed{}$

6 $40 + 10 = \boxed{}$

7 $70 + 10 = \boxed{}$

Write the partners.

1.

5   5   5   5

Write the partners and total for each circle drawing.

2. ☐ + ☐

●●●●● ○○○○○

Total ☐

3. ☐ + ☐

●●●●● ●● ○○

Total ☐

Show your work. Use drawings, numbers, or words.

Solve the story problem.

4. 5 chicks are in the coop. Some more chicks join them. Now there are 9 chicks. How many chicks join?

☐ _____
label

chick

5. **Stretch Your Thinking** What number is 5 tens and 10 ones? Write the number. Draw to explain.

Introduction to Tens Groupings

Name _____

Write how many.

1 **2**   **3** **4** **5**

[ ]   [ ]   [ ]   [ ]   [ ]

Find the unknown total or partner.

6 10 + 6 = [ ]   **7** 10 + [ ] = 18

8 10 + 1 = [ ]   **9** 10 + [ ] = 15

Start at 10. Count. Write the teen numbers.

10 | 10 | [ ] | [ ] | 14 |

| [ ] | [ ] | 17 | [ ] | [ ] |

Name _____

Write the partners and the switched partners.

1 8-train

+	+	+	+
+	+	+	+

Write the partners and the total. Then write the equation.

2 [ ] + [ ]

_____
Equation

Total [ ]

Add 1 ten.

3 60 + 10 = [ ]   **4** 20 + 10 = [ ]

5 80 + 10 = [ ]   **6** 50 + 10 = [ ]

7 70 + 10 = [ ]   **8** 30 + 10 = [ ]

9 Stretch Your Thinking If $10 + 7 = 17$,
then what is $20 + 7$? Draw to explain.

$20 + 7 = $ [ ]

Explore Teen Numbers

Name _____

Write how many.

1

2

3

4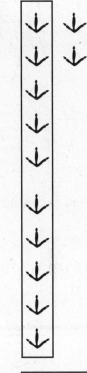

Find the total.

5 $10 + 9 =$ [ ]

6 $10 + 4 =$ [ ]

7 $10 + 2 =$ [ ]

8 $10 + 8 =$ [ ]

9 $10 + 6 =$ [ ]

Write the teen number.

10 | ○ ○ ○ ○ ○ [ ]

11 | ○ ○ ○ ○ ○
     ○ ○ ○ ○ [ ]

12 | ○ ○ ○ ○ ○
     ○ ○ [ ]

Find the unknown partner.

1  **2** 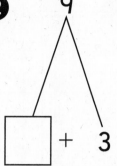 **3** 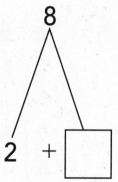 **4**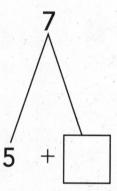

Write how many.

5  **6** 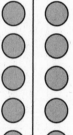 **7** 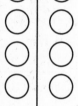 **8**

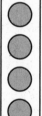

9 **Stretch Your Thinking** Write or
draw two different ways to
show the number 13.

Represent and Compare Teen Numbers

Name _____

Write an equation for the drawing. Then make a ten.

1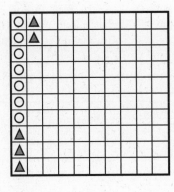

7 + _____

10 + _____

2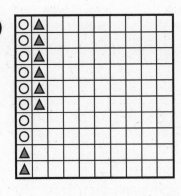

_____

_____

3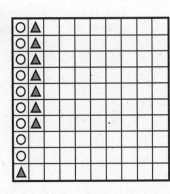

_____

_____

4 Emily has a box of 10 soaps and 4 extra soaps. How many soaps does she have?

soap

[ ] _____
   label

Find the total.

5 7 + 6 = [ ]   **6** 9 + 6 = [ ]   **7** 8 + 4 = [ ]

8   6   **9**   9   **10**   7
     + 5   + 8   + 7

1 Write the 10-partners and the switched partners.

⬤⬤⬤⬤⬤ ⬤⬤⬤⬤⬤ ⬤⬤⬤⬤⬤ ⬤⬤⬤⬤⬤ ⬤⬤⬤⬤⬤
⬤⬤⬤⬤◯ ⬤⬤⬤◯◯ ⬤⬤◯◯◯ ⬤◯◯◯◯ ◯◯◯◯◯

$\underline{9+1}$ $\underline{\quad+\quad}$ $\underline{\quad+\quad}$ $\underline{\quad+\quad}$ $\underline{\quad+\quad}$

$\underline{1+9}$ $\underline{\quad+\quad}$ $\underline{\quad+\quad}$ $\underline{\quad+\quad}$ $\underline{\quad+\quad}$

Count on to find the unknown partner.

2 $5 + \boxed{} = 8$ **3** $6 + \boxed{} = 9$ **4** $5 + \boxed{} = 10$

Count on to solve.

5 $\begin{array}{r} 9 \\ -5 \\ \hline \end{array}$ **6** $\begin{array}{r} 7 \\ -3 \\ \hline \end{array}$ **7** $\begin{array}{r} 10 \\ -9 \\ \hline \end{array}$ **8** $\begin{array}{r} 6 \\ -4 \\ \hline \end{array}$

Write the teen number.

9 ◯ ◯ ◯ ◯ $\boxed{}$

10 ◯ ◯ ◯ ◯ ◯
◯ $\boxed{}$

11 **Stretch Your Thinking** Choose a teen total. Write three equations that show different partners for your total.

_____ _____ _____
Equation   Equation   Equation

© Houghton Mifflin Harcourt Publishing Company

Visualize Teen Addition

Solve the story problem.

Show your work. Use drawings, numbers, or words.

1 There are 5 boys inside the tent and 8 boys outside the tent. How many boys are there?

tent

☐ _____
    label

2 I caught 9 fish yesterday. I catch 7 fish today. How many fish do I catch in all?

fish

☐ _____
    label

Find the teen total.

3 8 + 7 = ☐   **4** 9 + 3 = ☐   **5** 4 + 8 = ☐

6 9 + 6 = ☐   **7** 8 + 8 = ☐   **8** 8 + 9 = ☐

9 7 + 7 = ☐   **10** 5 + 7 = ☐   **11** 6 + 5 = ☐

Count on to find the total.

1 2 + 5 = ☐   **2** 4 + 2 = ☐   **3** 3 + 7 = ☐

4 6 + 4 = ☐   **5** 3 + 5 = ☐   **6** 5 + 4 = ☐

Count on to find the unknown partner.

7 6 + ☐ = 9   **8** 8 + ☐ = 10   **9** 5 + ☐ = 10

10 5 + ☐ = 8   **11** 4 + ☐ = 7   **12** 7 + ☐ = 9

Write an equation for the drawing. Then make a ten.

13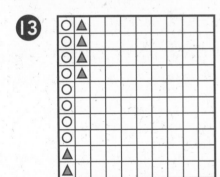

_____

_____

14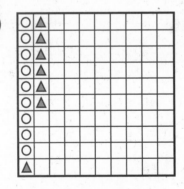

_____

_____

15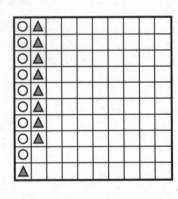

_____

_____

16 **Stretch Your Thinking** Write a story
problem for 9 + 5 = ☐. Solve it.

_____

_____

Teen Addition Strategies

Name _____

Find the total.

1 9 + 9 = ☐   **2** 5 + 5 = ☐   **3** 8 + 8 = ☐

4 7 + 7 = ☐   **5** 10 + 10 = ☐   **6** 6 + 6 = ☐

Use a double to find the total.

7 6 + 8 = ☐   **8** 8 + 9 = ☐   **9** 7 + 6 = ☐

10 5 + 6 = ☐   **11** 7 + 9 = ☐   **12** 5 + 4 = ☐

13 7 + 5 = ☐   **14** 7 + 8 = ☐   **15** 6 + 4 = ☐

16 9 + 8 = ☐   **17** 8 + 7 = ☐   **18** 8 + 10 = ☐

19 8 + 6 = ☐   **20** 6 + 5 = ☐   **21** 9 + 10 = ☐

22 6 + 7 = ☐   **23** 9 + 7 = ☐   **24** 5 + 7 = ☐

Name _____

Underline the greater number.
Count on from that number.

1 2 + 8 = ☐

2 7 + 3 = ☐

3 5 + 2 = ☐

4 4 + 5 = ☐

Solve the story problem.

Show your work. Use drawings, numbers, or words.

5 Adam has 10 apples. 7 apples are
red and the rest are green.
How many apples are green?

apple

☐ _____
label

6 I read 8 books this week. I read
7 books last week. How many
books do I read in all?

book

☐ _____
label

7 **Stretch Your Thinking** Look for a pattern.
Find the double of 11.

8 + 8 = 16

9 + 9 = 18

10 + 10 = 20

11 + 11 = ☐

Investigate Doubles

1 How many turtles?

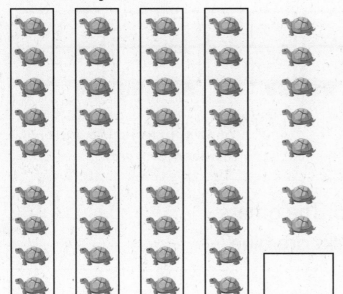

turtles

2 How many butterflies?

butterflies

Write the numbers.

3

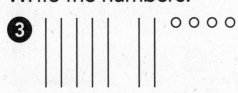

_____ = _____ tens _____ ones

4

_____ = _____ tens _____ ones

5

_____ = _____ tens _____ ones

Draw 10-sticks and circles.

6 52

7 26

8 48

Name _____

Write the partners and the switched partners.

1 10-train

Solve the story problem.

Show your work. Use drawings, numbers, or words.

2 I have 9 masks. 4 are red. The others are blue. How many masks are blue?

mask

[ ] _____
      label

Use a double to find the total.

3 6 + 5 = [   ] | 4 9 + 8 = [   ] | 5 7 + 6 = [   ]

6 5 + 7 = [   ] | 7 7 + 9 = [   ] | 8 6 + 8 = [   ]

9 **Stretch Your Thinking** Tully draws four 10-sticks and less than ten circles to make a number. Write the numbers that Tully could make.

_____

_____

Understand Tens and Ones

Write the numbers.

1

_____ = _____ tens _____ ones

2

_____ = _____ tens _____ ones

Draw 10-sticks and circles.

3 81

4 27

Write the number. Ring the number word.

5

[ ]   two   twelve   twenty

6

[ ]   one   ten   eleven

7

[ ]   four   fourteen   forty

8

[ ]   three   thirteen   thirty

Underline the greater number.
Count on from that number.

1 5 + 2 = ☐

2 6 + 3 = ☐

3 3 + 7 = ☐

4 1 + 9 = ☐

Write the number.

5 ||||| ∘∘∘∘∘ ∘∘ ☐

6 |||| ∘∘∘∘ ☐

Draw 10-sticks and circles.

7 82

8 39

Solve the story problem.

Show your work. Use drawings, numbers, or words.

9 Aria has 10 dolls. She gives 5 of them away. How many dolls are left?

☐ _____
label

doll

10 **Stretch Your Thinking** Sue says the drawing shows 35. Liam says the drawing shows 53. Ring the tens. Underline the ones. Write the correct number.

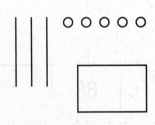

Integrate Tens and Ones

Write the number.

1 | | | | | | ○ ○

[   ]

2 | ○ ○ ○ ○ ○ ○ ○

[   ]

Draw 10-sticks and circles.

3 73

4 19

Draw 10-sticks and circles. Write the number shown.

5 [   ] = 30 + 4

6 [   ] = 50 + 6

7 [   ] = 40 + 1

8 [   ] = 60 + 5

Write the next number.

9 | 38 | 39 | [   ] |

10 | 58 | 59 | [   ] |

11 | 88 | 89 | [   ] |

12 | 48 | 49 | [   ] |

Name _____

Count on to solve.

1 $8 - 4 =$ ☐   **2** $10 - 7 =$ ☐   **3** $9 - 5 =$ ☐

4 $\begin{array}{r} 9 \\ -\ 6 \\ \hline \end{array}$ **5** $\begin{array}{r} 7 \\ -\ 5 \\ \hline \end{array}$ **6** $\begin{array}{r} 10 \\ -\ 8 \\ \hline \end{array}$

Write the number. Ring the number word.

7 | | | | | | | | | ☐   eight   eighteen   eighty

8 | ○ ○ ○ ○ ○ ○ ○   ☐   seven   seventeen   seventy

Find the total. Then make a ten.

9 $8 + 7 =$ ☐

$10 +$ ☐ $=$ ☐

10 $5 + 9 =$ ☐

$10 +$ ☐ $=$ ☐

11 **Stretch Your Thinking** What number is 1 more than 99? Draw to show how you know.

☐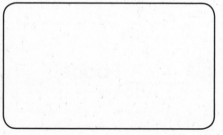

Practice Grouping Ones into Tens

Name _____

Each jar has 10 beans. How many beans are there?

1

2

3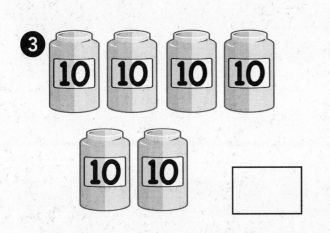

4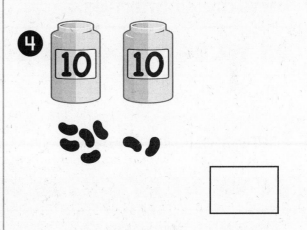

Each box in the bagel shop holds 10 bagels.
Draw to solve the story problem.

5 There are 7 boxes and
4 extra bagels. How
many bagels are there?

☐ bagels

6 There are 3 boxes and
8 extra bagels. How
many bagels are there?

☐ bagels

1 Write the numbers from 1–20.

1	2					7			
11			14						

Solve. Write how many are left.

2 There are 8 butterflies.

Then 5 fly away.

$8 - 5 = \boxed{}$

3 There are 10 turtles.

Then 8 crawl away.

$10 - 8 = \boxed{}$

Write the next number.

4 | 78 | 79 | |
5 | 48 | 49 | |

6 | 88 | 89 | |
7 | 68 | 69 | |

8 **Stretch Your Thinking** Choose and ring a way to solve $6 + 7$. Then draw to show your work.

count on

make a ten

doubles plus 1

Add with Groups of Ten

Each box has 10 crayons. How many crayons are there?

1 10 10 10 10

[crayons] [crayons] ☐

2 10 10 [crayons]

10 [crayons] ☐

3 10 10 10 10

10 10 [crayons] ☐

4 10 10 10 10

10 [crayons] ☐

Write the numbers.

Draw 10-sticks and circles.

5 | | | | | | ○ ○ ○ ○

____ = ____ tens ____ ones

7 34

6 | | ○ ○ ○ ○ ○
○ ○ ○

____ = ____ tens ____ ones

8 62

Name _____

1 Write how many dots. See the 5 in each group.

☐ ☐ ☐ ☐ ☐

Solve the vertical form. Use any method.

2 4
  +5

3 3
  +7

4 9
  +1

5 1
  +9

6 5
  +2

7 3
  +3

8 3
  +5

9 1
  +8

10 4
  +6

11 4
  +4

Each jar has 10 beans. How many beans are there?

12

☐

13

☐

14 **Stretch Your Thinking** Draw a new problem like Exercise 13. Show groups of ten and extras. Write the number.

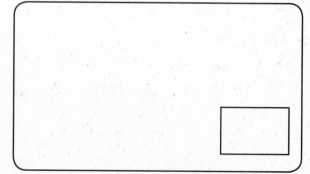

Practice with Tens and Ones

Name _____

Compare the numbers.
Write >, <, or =.

1 ‖ ∘∘∘∘∘ ‖‖‖ ∘

25 ◯ 41

2 ‖‖ ∘∘∘∘∘ ‖‖‖ ∘∘
   ∘∘

37 ◯ 32

3 46 ◯ 46   **4** 80 ◯ 79   **5** 30 ◯ 40

6 84 ◯ 93   **7** 51 ◯ 37   **8** 61 ◯ 16

9 44 ◯ 4   **10** 75 ◯ 75   **11** 56 ◯ 57

Compare the numbers two ways.
Write the numbers.

12 Compare 18 and 21.

___ ___ ◯ ___ ___

___ ___ ◯ ___ ___

13 Compare 76 and 67.

___ ___ ◯ ___ ___

___ ___ ◯ ___ ___

14 Compare 42 and 43.

___ ___ ◯ ___ ___

___ ___ ◯ ___ ___

15 Compare 50 and 95.

___ ___ ◯ ___ ___

___ ___ ◯ ___ ___

Subtract and write the equation.

1    _____
                                              Equation

Subtract 4

2    _____
                                              Equation

Subtract 6

Solve. Watch the signs.

3 $5 + 5 = \boxed{}$ **4** $8 + \boxed{} = 9$ **5** $\boxed{} + 4 = 8$

6 $8 - 4 = \boxed{}$ **7** $10 - \boxed{} = 7$ **8** $\boxed{} - 2 = 7$

Write the number.

9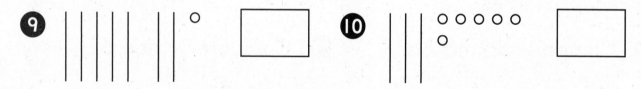

11 **Stretch Your Thinking** Write a number
that is greater than 55 and less than 65.

Add.

1 4 + 2 = ☐   40 + 20 = ☐

2 3 + 5 = ☐   30 + 50 = ☐

3 6 + 3 = ☐   60 + 30 = ☐

4 2 + 5 = ☐   20 + 50 = ☐

5 50 + 1 = ☐   50 + 10 = ☐

6 80 + 1 = ☐   80 + 10 = ☐

7 Each can has 10 peaches. How many peaches are there in all?

☐ peaches

Solve the story problem.

Show your work. Use drawings, numbers, or words.

1 Noah sees 10 turtles. Some turtles swim away. Now there are 4 turtles. How many turtles swim away?

turtle

☐ _____
          label

Find the unknown partner.

2 $5 + \boxed{} = 6$ **3** $8 + \boxed{} = 9$ **4** $6 + \boxed{} = 10$

5 $8 + \boxed{} = 10$ **6** $5 + \boxed{} = 8$ **7** $2 + \boxed{} = 7$

Compare the numbers.
Write <, >, or =.

8 28 ◯ 28   **9** 18 ◯ 81   **10** 34 ◯ 36

11 97 ◯ 79   **12** 53 ◯ 53   **13** 60 ◯ 59

14 **Stretch Your Thinking** Choose a number between 25 and 37. Write your number. Add a ten. Then add another ten. Write the new number.

☐   ☐
My Number   New Number

Solve.

1 4 + 3 = _____

40 + 30 = _____

40 + 3 = _____

2 2 + 7 = _____

20 + 70 = _____

20 + 7 = _____

3 5 + 4 = _____

50 + 40 = _____

50 + 4 = _____

4 1 + 5 = _____

10 + 50 = _____

10 + 5 = _____

5 6 + 2 = _____

60 + 20 = _____

60 + 2 = _____

6 5 + 3 = _____

50 + 30 = _____

50 + 3 = _____

7 2 + 4 = _____

20 + 40 = _____

20 + 4 = _____

8 8 + 1 = _____

80 + 10 = _____

80 + 1 = _____

9 Each box has 10 crayons.
How many crayons are there in all?

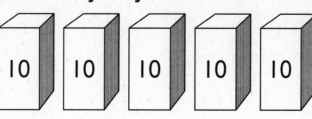 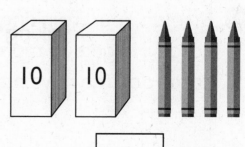

_____ crayons

1 Write the numbers from 1–20.

1									
11									

Count on to find the unknown partner.

2 $5 + \boxed{} = 9$

3 $8 + \boxed{} = 10$

4 $7 + \boxed{} = 8$

5 $4 + \boxed{} = 7$

6 $7 + \boxed{} = 10$

7 $2 + \boxed{} = 5$

Add.

8 $2 + 6 = \boxed{}$ $20 + 60 = \boxed{}$

9 $7 + 2 = \boxed{}$ $70 + 20 = \boxed{}$

10 $50 + 1 = \boxed{}$ $50 + 10 = \boxed{}$

11 **Stretch Your Thinking** Lucas has 5 trading cards. He gets 30 more cards. How many cards does he have now?

$\boxed{}$ cards

Mixed Addition with Tens and Ones

Find the total.

1 38 + 4 = ☐   **2** 42 + 5 = ☐   **3** 56 + 7 = ☐

4 78 + 2 = ☐   **5** 60 + 8 = ☐   **6** 15 + 4 = ☐

7 59 + 3 = ☐   **8** 92 + 6 = ☐   **9** 81 + 5 = ☐

10 12 + 5 = ☐   **11** 23 + 7 = ☐   **12** 64 + 7 = ☐

Count. Write the numbers.

13

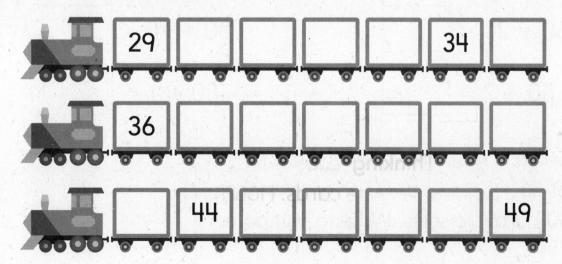

| 29 | | | | | 34 | |

| 36 | | | | | | |

| | 44 | | | | | 49 |

Solve. Watch the signs.

1 2 + 5 = ☐

2 6 + ☐ = 10

3 ☐ + 8 = 10

4 9 − 4 = ☐

5 10 − ☐ = 1

6 ☐ − 6 = 1

Write the number.

7 ☐

8 ☐

Draw 10-sticks and circles.

9 25

10 58

Solve.

11 5 + 2 = ☐

 50 + 20 = ☐

 50 + 2 = ☐

12 8 + 1 = ☐

 80 + 10 = ☐

 80 + 1 = ☐

13 **Stretch Your Thinking** Is the total of 86 + 5 less than 90 or greater than 90? Draw to solve. Write to compare.

Counting On Strategy: 2-Digit Numbers

Find the total. Use any method.

1 $57 + 6 =$ ☐

2 $32 + 8 =$ ☐

3 $76 + 5 =$ ☐

4 $15 + 2 =$ ☐

5 $90 + 9 =$ ☐

6 $65 + 7 =$ ☐

7 $79 + 3 =$ ☐

8 $58 + 4 =$ ☐

9 $67 + 9 =$ ☐

10 $89 + 1 =$ ☐

Compare. Write >, <, or =.

11 78 ◯ 80

12 41 ◯ 40

13 91 ◯ 9

14 37 ◯ 56

Solve the story problem.

Show your work. Use drawings, numbers, or words.

1 There are 7 children in the yard. Then 3 more children come. How many children are in the yard now?

child

[ ] _____
label

Write the number.

2 ||||| ○○○○○○ ○○ [ ]

3 |||||| ○○○○ [ ]

Draw 10-sticks and circles.

4 91

5 36

Find the total. Use any method.

6 30 + 6 = [ ]   **7** 50 + 9 = [ ]   **8** 91 + 5 = [ ]

9 79 + 2 = [ ]   **10** 28 + 6 = [ ]   **11** 47 + 8 = [ ]

12 **Stretch Your Thinking** Ella has 65 photos. Dan has 78 photos. Who has more photos? Explain.

_____

_____

Practice with 2-Digit Numbers

Count on to add.

1 48 + 3 = ⬜

2 72 + 4 = ⬜

3 69 + 4 = ⬜

4 30 + 9 = ⬜

5 50 + 7 = ⬜

6 86 + 5 = ⬜

7 36 + 2 = ⬜

8 47 + 6 = ⬜

9 23 + 5 = ⬜

10 59 + 7 = ⬜

11 ⬜ = 12 + 6

12 ⬜ = 60 + 9

13 ⬜ = 39 + 3

14 ⬜ = 49 + 1

15 ⬜ = 22 + 7

16 ⬜ = 65 + 9

1 Write the numbers from 1–20.

1									
11									

Solve the story problem.

Show your work. Use drawings, numbers, or words.

2 Matt has 8 seeds to plant in a red pot and a blue pot. How many seeds can he plant in each pot? Show two answers.

seeds

☐ seeds in the red pot and ☐ seeds in the blue pot

or ☐ seeds in the red pot and ☐ seeds in the blue pot

Find the total. Use any method.

3 $48 + 6 = $ ☐

4 $39 + 4 = $ ☐

5 $77 + 7 = $ ☐

6 $85 + 9 = $ ☐

7 **Stretch Your Thinking** Draw 10-sticks and circles to show the number that is 1 more than 89. Write the number.

☐

2-Digit Addition Games

Draw to show each number.

1 There are 20 boys and girls in a show.
There are more girls than boys.

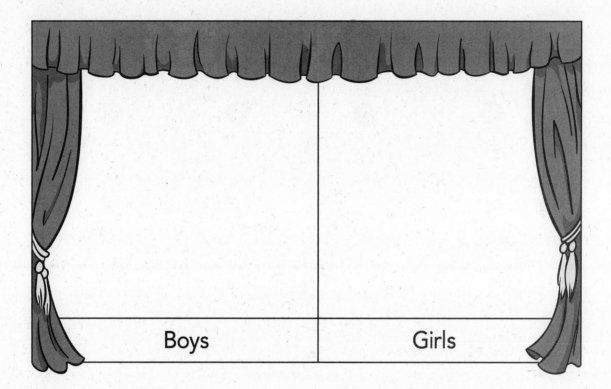

Boys   Girls

Write the number.

2 How many boys?   **3** How many girls?

[ ]   [ ]

Compare the numbers in two ways.

4 [ ] > [ ]   [ ] < [ ]

Name _____

Add.

1   4
     + 3

2   6
     + 2

3   8
     + 1

4   5
     + 5

5   2
     + 4

Subtract.

6   10
     − 4

7   8
     − 5

8   9
     − 8

9   7
     − 1

10   10
      − 3

Count on to add.

11 $20 + 9 =$ ☐

12 $87 + 3 =$ ☐

13 $68 + 6 =$ ☐

14 $25 + 8 =$ ☐

15 ☐ $= 79 + 6$

16 ☐ $= 56 + 5$

17 **Stretch Your Thinking** Write a number greater than 19 in Box A. Write a number less than 99 in Box B. Compare your numbers.

Box A   Box B

           Focus on Mathematical Practices